Up the Down Street

Nora Bates

Adare Press

ADARE PRESS
White Gables
Ballymoney Hill
Banbridge
Telephone: (08206) 23782

Dedicated to the memory of my husband and parents

ACKNOWLEDGEMENT

Thanks are due to the National Trust for permission to reproduce photographs of Rowallane House, Gardens and the Armytage Moores.

Thanks for help and encouragement are due to Francis Bailey and Mike Snowdon, Laura McIlhennon Rogers Dickie, Dick Newell, Jeffrey Kelly, Doreen McBride, Dr. Joy Higginson, my husband Ernest, daughters Gillian and Nicola and also to Gary Shaw for the illustrations and for designing the cover.

Published by Adare Press
Typeset by December Publications
Printed by Banbridge Chronicle

ISBN 1 899496 00 9

CONTENTS

William John and Annie Davidson, Saintfield, Co. Down. William John died 1969, wife Annie died 1979.
The above are the parents of Nora Bates.

IN THE BEGINNING

I was born in March 1934 and later discovered I was part of a large family, eight sisters and four brothers. My birth was as welcome as holy water in an Orange Hall. Annie was my mother's name and my father was called William John Davidson. He worked as a rent collector for Colonel Price so our home in Down Street in the small village of Saintfield, County Down was rent free.

We lived in the poverty stricken part of Saintfield, Downpatrick Street. My late father used to call it 'Downing Street' although we certainly did not have the luxuries of 'No. 10'. The houses were known as a 'two up, two down' that is, two rooms upstairs and two rooms downstairs. They had few amenities such as running water and a bathroom was an unheard of luxury. It's still hard to believe that my mother reared 13 children there.

Winters were very cold. We used to take a brick out of the oven, wrap it in an old piece of cloth and put it into bed to act as a hot water bottle. We were short of blankets so we threw our coats over the bed, a common practice. People use to talk about 'blankets with pockets'!

Most of our home life centred around the old range in the kitchen. The smell of my mother's cooking still floats into my nostrils. She used to send us to the butcher's to buy a marrow bone. The bone was placed in a large pot on the range. Mother added salt, pepper, water, barley and available vegetables, then left it to simmer and flavour. Many times I have tried to capture the smell and the taste but have never succeeded.

Our house was in a bad state of repair. We did not have a toilet, so we used the 'dung hill'. In later years my father built a small shed out of grey bricks and fitted it with a tin bucket.

At school I made friends with another girl. Next day she told me she was not allowed to play with me. I asked why? She said her mother had told her we did not bath or wash our clothes. How could we with no running water and no toilet facilities?

There were two schools in Saintfield, one for Protestants, the other for Catholics. I started to attend the Protestant one in 1940. I remember the teacher of the infants' class, Miss Stevenson, a petite spinster with her hair swept severely back. She looked cold but was caring and kind hearted, giving us attention and love which was not available at home.

Our classroom was small with four rows of desks and chairs. We sat there quietly doing our sums and spellings. Miss Stevenson always took time and care explaining difficulties and guiding us in many ways.

I remember Miss Stevenson putting her arm around me and making me feel safe and protected. She never used corporal punishment. She was unique and made a great impression on me as I came from a family which did not show physical affection, this lady's caring personality became important and has stayed with me right through my life. I feel she influenced my decision to go into nursing. It was almost as if her hand guided my decision.

The next teacher was memorable too but for totally different reasons. Miss H. Hay had the classroom next to the principal's and we dreaded going to her. She used corporal punishment almost every day. This sadistic character possessed rulers of various sizes and a large stick! Few escaped her vicious bullying and I can still hear the swish of that stick. Many times

our legs were left bleeding after her beatings and our hands were so raw we couldn't hold a pencil properly. The awful thing was knowing I was at her mercy. I could never understand why no one in authority, parents or guardians, considered challenging her attitudes and actions. I remember her clearly. She was large and plump and as children we somehow connected her moods with the colour of her clothes. We were frightened and wary when she wore yellow and were extra careful about what we did and said!

How overjoyed we were when we finally made the last move up to the class of the master, Victor Coulter, the last move. My memories of this teacher are very vague. He did not make much of an impression on me. He was reserved, mild tempered and of average height with nothing special about him. I do recall he was not averse to using the rod. Mr. Coulter died when I was still a child and all the children marched in rows at his funeral.

I was very short–sighted and became unable to see properly between ten and eleven years of age. When I told my parents they told me to ask the teacher if I could sit at the front of the classroom. I was moved to the front but was still unable to see the blackboard although this did not seem to bother the teachers and I missed out on a large part of my education, such as it was. The National Health Service was unheard of in 1944. After it was introduced in 1947 I got my first pair of glasses.

They came in blue for boys and pink for girls. I remember the optician saying "I don't know how you managed to cross the road without killing yourself!"

We were regular churchgoers. The vicar was called Reverend Charles Gorman and later I remember the Reverend James Donnelly. They both had children about my age but they did not attend my school!

A typical Sunday in the 1930's and 1940's included Sunday School at 10 am., held in the Parish Hall, Comber Road, then on to the "big church" for morning service. If the choir numbers were low we filled the empty spaces, then we returned home for dinner and afterwards were allowed to go for a stroll. Only the 'other side' that is the Catholics, had any organised Sunday entertainment. We usually visited the beautiful gardens at Rowallane. The owner, Mr. Armytage Moore encouraged locals to come in and enjoy his gardens and there was no charge for Saintfield people.

Afternoon tea was followed by the 6.30 pm church service. At the end of the service the vicar disappeared. He did not stand at the door and shake hands as most clergy do today. The vicar's wife always stood in the doorway chatting to people but I never remember her talking to children. We arrived home at 8.30 pm., listened to the wireless, then went off to bed ready for school next day.

The church organised a youth club up at the old vicarage and we often attended. It was a lovely old house, no longer connected with the church. Traipsing up the little lane we took part in many activities, welcoming tea and biscuits for our supper. We were lucky we had somewhere to go as our house was always crowded and noisy and, speaking personally, I always enjoyed glimpses of the type of life possible away from the grinding poverty of Down Street.

PEOPLE OF DOWN STREET

Most of the houses were on the left of old Down Street. We lived at the brow of the hill in a terrace which was separated by a crumbling lane from the neighbouring houses. The landlord never repaired the lane so it, like the house, was in a sorry state. It led round the back to the smelly dry toilets and the orange lilies Willie McGreevy grew for the celebrations which took place on the twelfth of July.

A slope led from the front doors of the terrace houses to the road. It was covered with sharp rocks and stones. We often tripped and were cut by the sharp edges. Cuts were simply washed under the water from the pump when often they should have been properly cleaned and sutured. Proper medical attention was too expensive for the poor like us so today there are many people who bear scars caused by falls in Down Street.

When the weather was fine we sat out on the rocks and talked or played games on the road. Cars were a rarity in those days so street games were safe. We swung round the lamp pole on a piece of rope, bounced a ball or played 'tig', a game where the person who was 'on' had to run and touch someone else who was then 'on'. It was fun.

Sometimes Mr. Armytage Moore, the owner of Rowallane which now belongs to the National Trust, drove up Down Street in his dark blue standard car. As soon as we heard it we would stand at the side of the road watching in silence and wonder. The car almost came to a standstill as it climbed the hill. We stood rigid and waved as if to royalty. He was always

My mother Annie, Granny Walkinshaw, Aunt Alice, Aunt Margaret and cousins in Down Street

alone and he waved and smiled at us. We went back to our games when he disappeared from view and I little thought that some day I should work in Rowallane.

The McClenaghan family lived next door on our right while John and Aggie lived to the left, with their daughters Lily and Sadie. Next to them lived William and his old mother who spent her days lying in bed looking out the small window at the back of the only downstairs room. Their front door was nearly always open, leaving the half door in place. They had a beautiful white cat which spent its days sitting on the half door.

My uncle, his wife and five children lived next door to John and Aggie while Cassie and Maggie lived in a tiny house round the corner. Maggie was bedridden and could not be left alone so Cassie often paid me to sit with her while she went shopping. I saved any money I earned to pay for trips into Belfast to visit an aunt.

James Kennedy lived with his brother Arthur and sister Maggie. None of the Kennedys ever married.

Maggie was a dressmaker. We used to enjoy helping with her housework. Sometimes we were allowed to make butter using her wooden churn. She always gave us share of her butter.

Whenever Maggie came to visit our house, she rapped the

door and asked, "May I come in, if I like?" One day Mum and Dad were out and we had another neighbour in the house. When Maggie made her usual request he shouted, "You may go to hell if you like!"

Poor James became very ill and died.

When anyone died in the street everyone visited the house to show sympathy for the living and respect for the dead.

My friend, Heather, and I decided to go after school. It never entered our heads to feel afraid or nervous.

Heather and I arrived at the house. Maggie invited us in and we shook hands with her. "We're sorry for your trouble," we mumbled. She was busy so asked us to sit down for a few minutes on the sofa. She finished making up the fire and filling the kettle and then said she was ready to take us up to see James in his coffin.

The bare wooden stairs led straight from the kitchen. Maggie went up first. We walked behind her. Our feet made a loud hollow sound on the bare boards which creaked and squeaked with every step. It seemed ages before we reached the small landing. Another two steps and we were in what seemed to us a large bedroom with a very high ceiling. The curtains were closed over the small window. The only light came from a small chink in the curtains. It was very dark.

A square of lino covered the wooden floor, an old fashioned chest of drawers stood in the corner. A small wicker table held a large basin and jug. A single dining room chair sat beside it.

We followed Maggie into the room. My friend started giving me nervous looks. I felt no fear. We moved over to where I could see a double bed with thick wooden panels at the top and bottom. At first all I saw was a dim shape in the bed. Then I saw the dazzling white linen sheets and bed cover. They were so white they appeared to sparkle. In those days people used to keep a special set of bed clothes to use at funerals. Maggie gently nudged us towards the bed. No words were spoken. I saw James's face. It was nearly as white as the bed clothes. I began to shiver. James was a Roman Catholic so had beads round his fingers and his hands were crossed on his chest. Maggie looked down at him, smiled, then told us to come down when we were ready and left.

Heather and I were transfixed. We stood there gazing at James for about ten minutes then slowly crept down the wooden stairs on our tip toes.

Maggie was busy working outside feeding the chickens and preparing to bring the cows from the town hill. We sat down in the kitchen and waited. We felt really shaken for a few minutes, then gradually recovered.

Eventually Maggie came back and poured two large mugs of lemonade and gave us three biscuits each. Sure that was what we had come for in the first place! We felt more cheerful. Sure death was just another occurrence, a part of living!

Paddy was a travelling salesman. He was a familiar sight in Down Street and a regular visitor to our house because Mum used to feed him. He was tall, well built and had a moustache. I really fancied the moustache!

Paddy travelled by train into Comber, Newtownards or Belfast, carrying household goods such as scrubbing brushes, clothes brushes, big wooden clothes pegs, tea aprons, men's socks and some ties. He packed his wares into a large brown case and walked miles around the countryside visiting farms and houses, selling the contents of his case.

We could always tell when Paddy was coming up the street from the sound of his feet. He had been in the forces and his feet hit the road in military style. He approached the door, stood to attention then came clip clap up the stone hall and sat down on the dining room chair, in the small alcove beside our big brown wireless. He set his case in the middle of the floor.

Once he had settled Mum brought him a large bowl of home made vegetable soup, a thick slice of bread and a big mug of tea and set them on a chair beside him. No matter how busy Mum was scrubbing clothes on the old fashioned wash board, making stew or preparing our evening meal, she always found time to feed him. Paddy removed his cap before eating. We looked upon him as a sort of uncle. Mum and he always had a long chat during which they exchanged news about people they both knew.

When he felt it was time to go Paddy jumped up, stood to attention, then moved to where his big brown case was sitting, turned it on its side, snapped the lid open and invited Mum to have a look. She examined his dish clothes, packets of buttons, brown and white laces and so on. She rarely bought anything but Paddy valued her opinion about how his goods would sell and their suitability for country folk.

Once Paddy must have bought a shop clearance because he produced a pair of children's shoes from the bottom of the case. They were wonderful! Brown and white crocodile skin

Mrs Martin outside her cabin in Down Street

with a strap and button. I longed for them but it was not to be.

Shortly afterwards, Paddy died a lonely death. He had been travelling around the country all day. He must have felt ill and weary. He made his way to an outhouse in a field, opened the door and just lay down. It was a cold night. The farmer found Paddy next day but he was already dead. He was truly a gentleman of the road and I have never forgotten him. He was sadly missed up the Down Street.

Joe Burton had a blacksmith's shop in the Down Street just past the New Line where my granny lived. He was a big friendly man, always talking and seldom without a customer. He wore a thick, long, black apron and his muscles rippled as he hammered at the forge. He was particularly busy on market days and at the Horse Fair when big and not so big horses took it in turns to have their shoes removed. The farmers swarmed up the street to Joe's forge. The horses' hooves went clip, clop, clip, clop on the road. Their owners were just as noisy with their heavy boots and trousers tied with twill at the ankles. Their rough tweed jackets hung loosely and there was not a Savile Row suit in sight.

Joe would cross over to the fire, take out the tongs and expertly lift the horse's foot. The smell was very strong and the air dense with steam and smoke. We used to peep in at Joe and listen to him talking to the animals, soothing the nervous and speaking sharply and firmly to the aggressive. He knew how to handle them all.

Every once in a while Joe came outside for a breath of fresh air, wiped his brow and sometimes yarned with a passing friend or neighbour.

The crack was good in the blacksmith's shop. There was a lot of laughing and spitting on hands or exchanging a good luck penny.

We were not allowed inside so spent the time bouncing our ball against the wall and listening to the crack. Looking back I think we were kept outside because of the danger from the big open fire.

Joe had a mind of his own about which jobs he wanted to do. Many a person brought metal to Joe and asked him to make something. Joe, if he was not in the mood, would take the metal in his hand as if judging the weight, walk to the forge door and appear to listen, turn round and throw the metal under the bench saying, "Sorry! Can't do it today. I have a horse to shoe." He would then start preparing for the arrival of an animal needing attention. The frustrated customer would be near the bottom of Down Street before he caught sight or sound of a horse.

Every June and December Joe closed the forge and went around the country collecting money owed to him by clients. Accounts were often settled over a dram of whiskey and Joe headed home in a merry mood with uncertain gait. Once he met the Rev. Stewart Dickson who called out "Drunk again, Joe!" "Yes!" came the reply in thick speech, "So Ah'm!"

Between 50 and 60 years ago counterfeit half–crown coins were being passed over the counter in Saintfield. The old half–crown has gone out of circulation. It was a heavy, solid silver coin which was a satisfactory weight in the hand. Nowadays it would only be worth twelve and a half pence but in those days it represented a fair bit of money.

The forgery started when one of the men from Down Street dressed in his best clothes and took his pretty little daughter, who was about five years of age at the time, to some of the wealthier homes in Saintfield just after the last train had left for Belfast. There was little, if any, communication between the rich and the poor so the man was not recognised as a local. He told a sob story about his daughter taking ill and causing him to miss his train and explained he did not have enough money to pay for a taxi. (He had a rail ticket to substantiate his tale.) People took pity on the wee girl and half–crowns were passed over for the taxi fare. The best half–crown was used to make moulds. Cutlery was bought from Woolworths, melted down, poured into the moulds and allowed to cool. The end result was a good quality forged half–crown.

The life style of a couple of men who lived in a house in Down Street changed dramatically. The police became suspicious and decided to watch their movements.

One afternoon one of the men was seen cycling towards Saintfield. Two policemen joined him and they cycled along together keeping each other in crack. One of the policemen quietly noticed the man was working something into his glove which he eventually dropped on the ground. The policeman picked it up and found a number of counterfeit half–crowns inside.

The police raided the suspected house and discovered all the equipment needed for a thriving money making business. The men concerned were arrested and served time.

There were a number of successful businesses around the village at that time but the half-crown manufacturer was the most successful.

Down Street was a close knit community and everyone was friendly and helpful. Money was in scarce supply but care and attention were plentiful. Anyone taking ill was fed soup and sweet milk by the neighbours. It was like a big united family and the people acted with compassion and dignity towards each other. The houses and facilities were in a sorry state but the people were wonderful.

LEARNING TO RIDE A BIKE

I used to help my cousin Alice with her paper round. I felt Alice was worldly wise and knew everything. One day I told her I would like to learn to ride a bike, a difficult undertaking as there appeared no possibility of either owning or borrowing one.

Alice, as usual, was full of good ideas. "People," she said, "who take the weekday train to Belfast, cycle in to the station and leave their bikes in the bicycle shed. That means there's a supply of bikes from about 9 a.m. to 5 p.m. every day of the week. We'll borrow a bike, I'll teach you to ride and we'll put it back. No harm done and nobody'll ever know!"

The big day arrived. We planned to borrow a bike after we had delivered the papers. We rushed down to the station but a signal man was standing at the top of the stairs outside the signal box. We stood around for about fifteen minutes, then decided to abandon our plan for the day.

We returned next day, but it was wet and windy. Alice insisted I needed good weather to make my debut on a bike. Next day we were back, but the Station Master was crossing the yard. He glowered at us and asked, "What do you want?" We said we had forgotten a bundle of papers.

At long last when we arrived at the station the weather conditions were good and we did not see a soul. We approached the bicycle shed and looked at the long row of bikes. "Nora, we'll need to pick a bike to fit you," said Alice. There were no ladies' bikes! We checked again. All the bikes were large and heavy with a thick iron cross bar. Should I give up my

ambition and perhaps learn at a later date? "No!" said Alice firmly. "You'll just have to learn on a man's bike!"

We pushed the heavy bike out of the station, expecting to hear shouts behind us demanding that we bring it back. When we were clear, we propped the bike up against a wall and breathed a sigh of relief, then stood and giggled. Alice wheeled the big bike into the middle of the road and helped me get my leg over the bar. I promptly fell over and we stood there laughing. Luckily there was very little traffic in those days. I tried again and managed to touch the pedals. "Pedal standing up," suggested Alice, "I'll hold the saddle and run along behind." I wobbled and lurched from side to side on the road. "Don't worry! Just keep going!" encouraged Alice.

I pedalled down to the end of the road and half fell off. We walked back and started all over again. "Boys! This is great!"

I thought. I was gaining confidence with every attempt.

We decided to have one last go and end the lesson for the day. As I went sailing and pedalling down the road, my hair and legs flying, I felt as free as a bird and so carefree. "Isn't this great?" I turned to Alice and realised she was standing at the top of the road cheering me on!

I glanced up and saw a red faced farmer bringing his cows to market. Then I found myself staring at a large red and white cow with big bulging eyes and a tail swishing from side to side. I panicked, wobbled and jerked on the road, pushed the handle bar to the left and fell into the ditch with the old bike on top of me. I felt my knickers rip and my legs sting from nettles. I cut my leg on a stone and the old farmer shouted at me.

Alice fished me out of the ditch, rubbed my stings with docken leaves and cleaned my cut. We took the bike back to the station to await its unsuspecting owner then we doubled up giggling and giggling. We could not stop, but I was able to handle a bike from that day on although I did not own one for another thirty years.

THURSDAYS IN HEAVEN

Every week on Thursday evenings the Church of Ireland youth club members were invited to the vicarage for a sort of social evening with the vicar and his children.

When we came back from school on Thursdays we finished our household jobs and homework quickly, rushed to do mother's messages, then spent the rest of the time getting ready and wondering what was in store for us. I must say we all looked forward to going and looked on it as a privilege and a treat. We thought we were lucky to be members of the Church of Ireland and we were extra obedient on Thursdays because we could be punished by not being allowed to go to the youth club and we had no intention of missing it.

When we set off from Down Street en route for the vicarage we turned left at the end of the street, walked the length of Main Street and into Lisburn Street where a narrow path led to the front of the house. We were terribly excited. I always fell silent when the house came into view and I approached what appeared to me to be a very large door with a big bell. Someone pulled the rope to ring the bell. Usually one of the vicar's children answered and let us in.

I always silently admired the old fashioned hall stand and mirror. It was here that umbrellas were left. I never had one! Then we were led into a large sitting room which had a lot of dark furniture. The ceilings were very high and as I glanced around this vast room I looked at all the photographs in silver frames of groups of children and of people, mostly old men, in black and white robes. I have no photographs of myself either

Fair View (Tea Row) on the way to the vicarage

as a child or as an adolescent.

Between 20 and 30 children attended the youth club. Some came from Down Street, others from Main Street and many from the townlands. Some of the children had new clothing with their hair nicely brushed and tied by ribbons. Oh! What I would have given for a bright dress that fitted and a pretty satin bow in my hair! I felt rejected and different. I could not understand why I could not have pretty things like some of the other children. The better dressed tended to stay together so we poor children were segregated.

The vicar had three children, Patrick, Helen and Kenneth. During the evening we were divided into three groups. One of the vicar's children led each group. We simply did whatever was suggested, following like sheep. It never entered our heads to suggest that one of us could lead a group.

I loved to feel the soft richness of the carpet under my feet. I felt as if I could have walked on that carpet for ever, as if I was treading on air. I always felt frightened in case I knocked against one of the lovely ornaments and broke it by accident and would not be allowed back.

One of the vicar's children would tell us to sit down, the Rev. Charles Gorman would be along shortly. As I sat down on the pale yellow arm chair with its thick upholstery and my thin legs dangled just off the floor I thought how lucky Patrick, Helen and Kenneth were to have this lovely room and the beautiful garden and how strange it was that they lived only a short distance from me. At times I prayed that God would make Da a bishop, or even a vicar, so that we could live in a place like this. After all, my Da was a good man and many people came to him for information, help and advice, perhaps more than went to the vicar. And Da never turned anyone away.

We sat in silence for what seemed ages until Rev. Gorman and his family came into the room. He read a short prayer and a passage from the Bible, then the games started! This was the real reason why we had come.

We divided into three groups. Funnily enough we stayed with people from our own area, the Down Street group, the Main Street group and the Townlands group. This just happened, it was not planned. Perhaps we felt most at ease with children we knew. We played snap, snakes and ladders, ludo and, if the weather was fine, we played rounders on the front lawn. We always ended with a quiz with the vicar's children writing down questions and us answering them.

One evening, before Rev Gorman came into the sitting room, I lifted my head and looked around. I gazed at the lovely lights hanging from the ceiling and the thick square carpet with its polished surround. Not one thing was out of place, except perhaps me. There were little linen clothes at the backs and arms of the chairs and settee. I touched one on the chair on which I was sitting. It felt nice as did the little fringe at the edge. I guess this was my first look and feel of Irish linen. I slowly climbed down from my armchair and began nervously walking around the room, looking first at the thick embossed wall paper and its lovely matching border. I silently and slowly made my way over to the large window and felt the rich green velvet curtains that reached down to the floor. I ran my hand up and down to feel their softness. I stopped at the corner of the room to admire the grandfather clock. I was careful not to go too near the wall and step on the highly polished surround around the carpet. I made my way towards the door and passed a huge brown sideboard with brass handles. I looked at the top. There were a lot of brass ornaments with a large bowl full to overflowing with apples and pears. I would have liked one. They smelt lovely. Behind the door was a thick red woollen curtain which matched the red and green carpet with its odd specks of yellow and white.

By about 8.30 a large tray of lemonade and a plate of biscuits was carried in by Helen and Kenneth. As I was given the long slim glass of home–made lemonade I had a terrible urge to put the glass to my lips and gulp the whole lot down in one go! I disciplined myself to drink slowly out of the grand glass. Then, when I had finished I rubbed my fingers up and down just to feel its rich texture. The large plate of biscuits was passed round. I looked at its cheery bright flowers and green leaves and thought it the most beautiful I had ever seen. Many's the time I slipped an extra biscuit and hid it in my pocket to enjoy later on! By the time we had finished eating and drinking it was time to go home. We walked slowly out into the hall and returned to reality, but oh, what bliss to go to heaven for two hours every Thursday.

A HAPPY CHRISTMAS AND A PROSPEROUS NEW YEAR

I knew Christmas was near when we started making paper decorations at school. I longed to bring some home but teacher always knew how many there were! We used crepe paper in a variety of colours, bright yellow, blues and dark red. They looked lovely and were soft to touch. It was a task we looked forward to each year.

We did not expect toys or clothes for Christmas or for birthdays. They were for other families.

My Aunt lived at the other side of the village. She came and told us when two of Saintfield's shops, Burgess and Marshall, decorated their windows about three or four weeks before Christmas. As soon as we knew the windows had been dressed we rushed down the street to have a look.

In those days the window displays had toys and household goods, such as tea sets and cutlery. There was always a crowd of adults and children around both windows but it was to Marshalls that I ran. I would press my face up against the window and gaze and gaze in wonder. Sometimes it was difficult to see the display as part of the window was covered in frost. I remember one display in particular, a toy monkey hanging from a rubber string in one corner. In the other there was a doll with a pink frilly dress and little white shoes. She had long curly hair and bright blue eyes. I could not bear to look away from those eyes. They seemed to be staring out just at me. I must have stood in the cold for hours. I glanced over at the Parish Church and sent up a silent prayer that Santa would bring me something. Anything would do. I did not dare to ask for the doll. Over the years I have often pondered about who was able to buy the toys and goods in the window. They were nearly all gone by Christmas

We had our own plans for Christmas. We went away up the Old Road and headed for Rowallane where we picked some wild holly and got a large holly bush for a tree. We saved silver milk bottle tops, punched holes in them and hung them on the tree with a piece of thread. We screwed up bits of coloured paper and put them on the tree and if we had a few extra pence we bought two ounces of chocolate drops from Mrs. Reid's and used them to grace the tree, although they disappeared by morning! Hazel painted a fairy, coloured it, cut it out and placed it at the top.

The only party we attended was the one run by the Sunday School in the parish hall, which, at that time, was down the Comber Road. There was a tree! A proper Christmas tree which looked enormous in the middle of the hall. I always walked round and round it looking at the tiny coloured lights, the gold and silver trimmings, the glistening fairy firmly attached to the top, unlike ours which kept falling down. There were funny little parcels in different colours hanging from every branch.

We drank orangeade, which was served in cups, ate sandwiches, buns, lots of buns, and every child from the church received a gift such as a game, sweets, or a Bible story book. I would have liked one of the parcels, a doll or a soft toy. There were a few there. I could see them. I turned away and thought, well, maybe next year!

Like all children we believed in Santa Claus. On Christmas Eve we hung a sock on the end of the bed. Somehow Santa always managed to bring a few sweets and a small toy for each child. We woke up early on Christmas Day, jumped out of bed and rushed to see what he had left. It was such a scramble! We always found a few sweets, sometimes a piece of fruit and sometimes, for fun, dad would fit in the chicken foot! Once I got a pirie and whip. The pirie was brown with bright green paint on top. I played with it for hours, treasured it and even took it to bed with me.

Mum got up first and set about lighting the big stove which stood in the middle of the kitchen and had a long pipe going into the wall. It took ages to get the fire going and even longer for the house to become warm.

As I came down the bare wooden stairs and my bare feet reached the freezing cold lino in the kitchen, I glanced at our Christmas tree which was sitting lopsided in its container in the corner. Some of the silver tops and coloured paper always seemed to fall off during the night but although it was only a holly bush I always thought it as big and grand as the tree in Trafalgar Square.

We pulled our clothes on in front of the fire, fetched a bucket of water from the pump, looked to see if the post man had brought any more cards and then went to see Granny, who lived down the New Line, to show her what Santa had brought. Then we went home again to get ready for church.

The church had plenty of decorations, flowers, holly and a lovely tree at the front. It always seemed cosy and warm. The service was simple, yet lovely. I always enjoyed listening to the Rev. Charles Gorman's brief sermon on Christmas morning and I loved singing the old carols.

After church Mum busied herself preparing the dinner. In those days poor folk could afford chicken at Christmas only so the bird was somewhat of a luxury. We ate potatoes and brussel sprouts with the chicken followed by custard and either tinned peaches or pears. Mum always made a large jelly in a jug and we ate every scrap of our food and enjoyed every minute. In the afternoon we were given a large slice of rich, moist dark fruit cake. It was lovely! By this time we had eaten most of our Christmas fare and there was little left. Nothing was wasted although we always managed to gather a few morsels for the dog. That old dog enjoyed Christmas as much as the children!

After dinner we visited our neighbours to see what Santa had brought. We wondered why he never responded to our letters. However, we thought we could do nothing about it. Santa would be safely back in Lapland. Many times I vowed I would write and complain next December when I pushed my note up the chimney. Others could have dolls and teddy bears. It was unfair. Perhaps my order had been mislaid or Santa had run out of money? We continued our tour of the houses in Down Street, chatting to our friends, playing snakes and ladders or ludo and sometimes telling each other ghost stories as of course there was no television in those days.

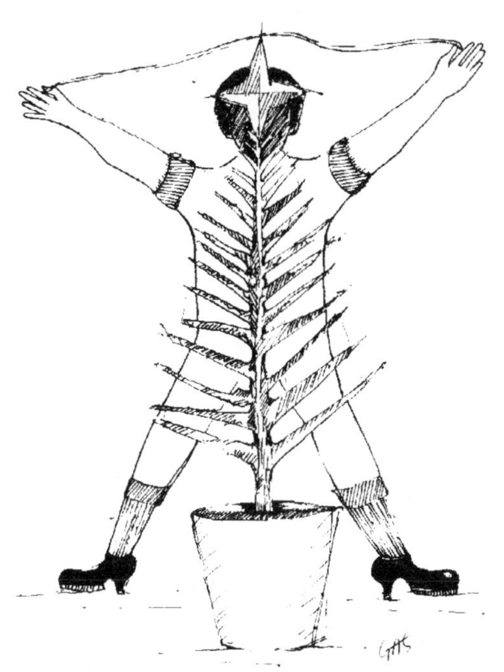

By this time it was getting dark and we

returned home for supper and ate any food which was left. My aunts visited us in the evening and the adults ate cold chicken, soda bread and biscuits and drank tea. Mum usually saved a few biscuits which she placed in a brown wicker basket which hung from a hook on the ceiling.

I fell asleep listening to voices and laughter. Another year and another Christmas had nearly gone. The next big event would be New Year's Day when I would have fun delivering wisps. A wisp was made from straw plaited into a braid about 3 (7 cms) inches wide and 10 inches (25 cms) long. Sometimes one of the ends was tied with ribbons, but usually they were tied with straw. That was cheaper. Da made us some wisps but did not have sufficient time to supply us all so Willie Sefton, John Mann and Jack Kelly also made them for us. Wisps were always made by men, never by women.

Now I realise that giving wisps on New Year's Eve was a remnant of a pagan custom ensuring fertility for the household for the following year, but in those days I just looked upon it as profitable fun. Wisps were hung up inside the house and were not taken down until replaced by a new one the following year. To remove one before then was considered very bad luck which few people would risk. At the time I felt I was simply bringing good luck to the house by delivering wisps and enjoying comparative prosperity in the form of luck pennies received in exchange.

Three or four of us walked together, carrying our wisps, down Main Street, the Comber Road, Todd's Hill and part of the Belfast Road. We did not do Down Street because most people had their own favourite 'wisp wishers' and we knew we would not be successful there.

I was fortunate because I had dark hair which was supposed to be lucky. On many occasions when I went to a door with a fair haired friend, who offered a wisp, the householder would say, "No thank you very much. I'll have a wisp from your friend", then reach over and take one from me. People with red or ginger coloured hair were supposed to be unlucky. Nobody would take a wisp from anyone of that colouring so redheads had to stay at home and miss all the fun.

We travelled from house to house, knocking on doors, and took it in turns to hold out a wisp as we wished the family, and home, "A Happy New Year." When we had given our greeting the wisp was accepted and we were given one or two pennies. Sometimes we struck lucky and were given three pennies! Riches indeed! Most of our clients looked out for us and appeared upset if they missed us. I cannot remember ever being refused when I offered a wisp on New Year's Eve.

One year the weather was fine and mild so we decided after we had 'wisped' the village we would go into the country and 'do' the farms. This meant a lot of walking along long lanes from farm to farm. We were made very welcome on our arrival at each farmhouse, were invited in a couple of times and given tea, soda bread and country butter. It was delicious. The bread was fresh and still warm, the butter round, bright yellow with a salty taste. It was plastered about an inch thick on the bread where it melted and ran down our chins. We seldom got cash at farms but were given presents such as a cabbage, a couple of turnips, a bag of potatoes or some nice fresh farm eggs. Gifts such as these were very welcome at home. We bought sweets or lemonade out of the money we collected or saved it until Friday night when Jim McKee made chips and we were able to have the small luxury of buying a bag. New Year's Eve was one of the few times we felt comparatively wealthy and I look back on our simple seasonal treats with pleasure.

THE TWELFTH

When I was a child I used to wonder how other countries and cultures managed to exist without our Twelfth of July celebrations. To children living in Down Street to be deprived of the "Twelfth" was unthinkable!

The eleventh night was fraught with excitement. Our house was full of folk coming and going, checking bus times, venues and other things like opening the Orange Hall. There was always a lot of crack with older folk reminiscing on events of yesteryear. My brothers were in Saintfield's Silver Band so there was a lot of cleaning of instruments and preparation of uniforms with the girls ironing trousers and shirts.

Ironing was a difficult feat because our old–fashioned iron was not powered by electricity, but by the fire. This meant we had to fish a rectangular piece of metal out of the iron, stick it into the fire until it became red hot, remove it, push it back into

Main Street practice for twelfth

the iron and smooth away until the iron became cold again, when we repeated the whole process. Frequently our hands became covered with burns.

It is amazing what sticks in the memory! I remember one eleventh of July when I was given six old pennies and sent to Davey Dodds, the butcher, to buy a marrow bone. My friend, Mary, came with me. We turned into Main Street, got as far as Steenson's, then looked to the right. A man was cycling towards us. We stood outside Peg Steenson's shop. The man came almost level with us, crossed over and got off his big bike with its big, black, bag on the back.

We watched in silence as the man removed the clips, which kept his wide grey trousers legs from becoming entangled in his bicycle chain. The man wore a hat and a black blazer. He glanced briefly in our direction as he was about to go into Gildea's. We just stared at him. He was a stranger. He hesitated for a split second, then came towards us. We tried to push our bodies into the wall behind us. He was very tall, yet he spoke with a soft voice. He asked how old we were and where we lived. I noticed he glanced at the ground with a mixture of concern and sadness. My friend was barefoot and I was wearing a big pair of shoes I had been given. I had filled them with newspaper to ensure a better fit. I have never forgotten his humanity as most people just brushed past us. I told my mother when I arrived home. She said I had been talking to the new minister of Second Saintfield Presbyterian Church, the Rev. William Dickie.

As a rule on the eleventh night around 7 pm several of us went for a walk. We visited neighbours and saw their preparations, the cleaning of instruments, clothes grooming and the important task of cleaning and mending the lodge banner and tying on black bows as a mark of respect if a

Saintfield accordion band

member had died during the year, and so on. We walked up the street admiring the Union Jack flags hanging from the majority of houses and the decorative arch over Main Street. There was a lot of joviality with small groups of people cracking about past years and small unofficial practise walks by bands playing. It was fun!

I do not remember bonfires ever being lit in Saintfield but I do have fond memories of the night we travelled into Belfast to see the bonfires there. Mollie and I were standing at the corner when Margaret and Jackie passed in their small car. They screeched to a stop, wound down the window and yelled "Would you like to see the bonfires in Belfast?" "Yes!" we shouted eagerly and climbed in.

Jackie drove through Carryduff to Belfast. It seemed like no time at all until we were down the Ormeau Road and in Donegall Pass. It was just before midnight, the whole of

Belfast appeared alight and there was a wonderful carnival atmosphere. The bonfires were huge and the crack was mighty! Saintfield appeared very quiet when we appeared home in the wee small hours of the morning.

On the morning of the "Twelfth" itself the girls got up early, lit the fire and had a quick cup of tea, then got out of the way so that the band members could titivate.

When I had finished drinking tea it was my job to lift the old heavy bucket and trudge across the street to the pump to get water. On the way back I always looked upwards and to my left. I liked to see the Union Jack Flag hanging from the upstairs window. Mother had made curtains out of yellow flour bags which she had dyed yellow with whin blossoms. If there was a breeze at all the curtains flew out of the window and wrapped themselves around the flagstaff. They became entwined with the flagstaff and waved proudly together. It was a strange sight!

About four of us always went up the street together and sat back to back on the large, grey, stone outside Mary's door. We chatted about our plans for the day and looked forward to the dance which followed the procession. Then we made our way down to the Orange hall to the bus which was waiting to take us to Ballynahinch, Comber or Ballygowan.

The bus was full of banners, instruments, drums and flags, so it was standing room only for children. Usually we were given a push and a shove up to the front by one of the officials. It was just great! We were full of pride and always had a marvellous day, rain or shine, walking about and chatting.

We arrived back in the village about 7 pm. The band completed the final march of the day and we made our way to the church hall for tea.

The church had a big silver urn. There were no tea bags in

those days so sufficient tea leaves were thrown into the urn along with milk and sugar and the whole lot was boiled. We drank the resulting sweet milky tea out of thick, white cups. It was too bad if anyone did not take milk or sugar because there was no choice. We ate big, thick sandwiches which were usually made from cornbeef although sometimes we had tomato instead. The sandwiches were so thick we called them "doorsteps". We were also given a small cake or biscuit as well.

The hall was tidied up after we had finished tea, the floor brushed and the dance commenced. We joined in and danced the 'lancers', 'foxtrot', 'waltzes' and all the other dances in vogue at the time. Mind you, by this time some of the brethren were quite merry and got the dances mixed up! We thought it was all good fun. The dance ended between 11 and 12 o'clock when the band played the national anthem. We could not help going into fits of giggles because some of the brethren drank so much they had difficulty standing up to attention while the national anthem was being played. Our giggles were rewarded by glares from sober lodge members.

On the road home we discussed the day's events and pitied those countries which had to survive without 'The Twelfth'?

GROWING UP

Subjects concerned with growing up were taboo during my youth. We found things out by chance and received a lot of misinformation. The natural processes of growing up were often confusing and frightening.

My feelings were suppressed. I had many sisters but never discussed my problems with them. It seemed no one had time to listen. I wondered why was I born? And what was my purpose in life? Others pretended to be happy and outgoing but deep down also had feelings of isolation, confusion and loneliness. They were very sad feelings.

I had an awful feeling of helplessness combined with a desire to crawl into a dark corner and hide because I had nothing to offer. I found it hard to accept myself and realise I did not have to go through life being a doormat for other people.

In our village a couple were sent to jail for neglecting their children. There were simple kindly folk and their home was always tidy. Their only crime was they did not have enough money to buy food and clothing. One day the authorities took

Brother Billy on bike in Down Street

the couple to Saintfield court and they were given a jail sentence. The children were taken into care. There was no welfare system and everybody in the Down Street felt the injustice of it.

Even though much of my childhood was dull and difficult I did have better moments! I had many friends in the street which, like most neighbourhoods, had its fair share of colourful characters. There were a brother and sister known as Miss Patterson and Matchbox Patterson (he was tall and skinny). They were eccentric but harmless. I remember the postman delivering two letters to the Patterson household. Miss Patterson called him back and returned one letter saying that one letter was enough at a time and that he could give her the other next day.

During summer evenings the children in the Down Street went out onto the road and played rounders, skipping and various other games. There was an old, well used, summer seat outside our house.

In the 30s and 40s there were no street lights. Evenings spent in the Street during October and November were cold, frosty and dark. We used to jump up and down to keep warm and we indulged in a lot of good natured horse play which took the form of pushing and shoving.

Jimmy lived in Down Street. We thought he was a bit odd, to put it mildly. One night, Rammy, a member of the gang had a bright idea. He produced a spool of black thread and explained he would like to play a trick on Jimmy. He sneaked across the road and tied the thread to Jimmy's door knocker then joined us hiding round the corner on the New Line. He tugged the thread and knocked the door. The door opened and Jimmy came out and looked round. It was so dark he was not able see the thread. After we had knocked his door several times he must have twigged that children were larking about. He appeared more and more irate and we were doubled up laughing. We pulled the thread once more and it broke. We crept up to tie it on again. Old Jimmy must have been standing behind the door listening. A bike came up the street with its light shining through the darkness. We looked up and beheld a glistening meat cleaver held in Jimmy's hand raised up above his head as he rushed out shouting at his invisible enemies, "If yous buggers don't clear off I'll kill yous! And if that doesn't stop yous I'll tell yer owl Das!"

We quickly took to our heels and scattered as we knew Jimmy, given half a chance, would have been capable of carrying out his threats!

As we grew more mature we became more sophisticated and no longer took part in street games. We stood at the corner and chatted. Sometimes we just joked but we often indulged in deep discussions about the general state of the cosmos and what the government should do, as well as sharing dreams of the future. It was through these early immature attempts at communication that we learnt how to mix and many a romance started at the street corner.

My school

BLACKBERRIES AND BEAUTY

At Hallowe'en evil spirits spit on blackberries and poison them, or so we believed. The blackberry season lasted a few weeks in the autumn and we really enjoyed excursions to pick them.

The time had to be just right for blackberry picking with the berries ready for pulling otherwise we had a wasted journey. We used a few old bushes along the garden hedge to test colour and size.

We set off early in the morning with a few soda farls covered with jam and a bottle of water for a picnic. Minnie, Ruby, Phoebe, Jean, Belle, Ivy and I had good crack on blackberry picking outings. It must have been possible to hear our laughter two or three fields away.

I remember Ivy and Jean talking about Mrs O'Hare who, they said, was 'expecting company'. Years later I realised her 'company' was a baby! This was how a lot of us discovered the 'facts of life'. There was a lot of talk about sex. We were told on no account to do 'IT', but did not know what not to do! Often when younger ones approached the older ones went quiet. This made us all the more curious! We were, however, offered advice and told not on any account to go with someone from 'the other side' (the Roman Catholic side of the population).

The older girls talked a lot about Friday and Saturday night dances they attended. They gossiped about who asked them to dance, the ones they 'clicked' and, most important, who had taken them home and if he was a 'good court' or not.

GAS

I was always anxious to hear more! We learnt how to set our hair with sugar and water and how to push it into waves with long clips. We discovered how to apply make–up 'expertly' using a long thick creamy pan stick on our faces. If we had no face powder, not to worry, a handful of flour would do! We must have looked lovely! Some one always managed to bring a few cigarettes and some matches. One day I remember asking Jean for a 'pull' and I promptly vomited. I did not try to smoke again for a long time!

Preparations for blackberry picking included taking the big heavy enamel bucket over to the pump, rinsing it out and collecting a small container each, usually a jam jar or an empty pea or pear tin. We put on our oldest clothes and foot wear because the blackberry thorns often became entangled with our clothes and tore them, as well as our arms and legs. Sometimes we would lean too far over in an attempt to reach tempting fruit, overbalance, spill the small container and end up scratched and torn in the middle of the bush.

We took turns at lugging the heavy bucket up the road. We walked miles along roads, then through fields, travelling deeper and deeper into the countryside, climbing over big iron gates. The gates were always locked and while it was comparatively simple throwing the bucket over on the outward journey it was a problem when laden with blackberries. One person climbed on to the top of the gate and the bucket was passed up. The person on top of the gate balanced the bucket on the top rung while another climbed over to the other side, reached for the bucket which was then passed down. Anybody dropping the bucket was in real trouble!

We often sang to keep our spirits up. Jean and Belle had particularly good singing voices and the fields and rocks vibrated with songs such as "She'll be coming round the mountains", "Wish me luck as you wave me goodbye", and "Now is the hour". Singing was very useful if one of us wandered too far away. The sound carried and acted as a guide back to the group. Sometimes there was a bull in a field and we had to make a hasty retreat!

We spent the whole day in the fields before wending our weary way home. We took it in turns to carry the empty bucket and every now and then would meet an acquaintance and gladly stop for a yarn. Eventually we reached Down Street and set about selling the berries. My father usually bought them and put them into big barrels to take to Miller's Jam Factory in East Belfast.

We were tired and hungry when we reached home and went to the street pump to wash our stained hands. It took ages to wash all the blackberry juice off. However, after a few days we forgot our weary limbs and the next time someone suggested going blackberry picking we were raring to go.

THE WHISTLING WOODCHOPPER AND OTHER GHOSTS

What was that? Terrified, we listened. It was the middle of the night. Someone was whistling. Did someone intend to murder us in our beds? Was it a burglar? We lay and trembled.

The noise changed. What was that? It sounded as if someone was hegging (chopping) sticks. Someone was whistling and hegging sticks in the middle of the night! The noise became louder and louder. It rose to a crescendo, woke the whole house, then died away after about ten minutes.

Next day we felt tired after our disturbed night. We grumbled to each other. "Fancy anyone hegging sticks at that time of the night." We forgot about the whole episode until it happened again about three weeks later.

Then two weeks later it happened again. Dad got up to investigate. He crept quietly out the back of the house and looked around the shed in which he kept Dolly the horse. He saw nothing.

The noise recurred again after about another two weeks. Again Dad investigated. Again he found nothing. The noise began to occur on a fairly regular basis, every two or three weeks. Dad looked for its source several times, but found nothing although he came to the conclusion that it always came from the same direction.

By this time the neighbours had begun to comment on the noise. They too tried to find its source to no avail. The whistling and hegging continued. Other folk began to talk and get curious and ask questions. Some of the men in the village

took it in turns to sit up and try and find the cause, but it was no use. Eventually on old man noticed a pattern. Someone died within 48 hours of each nocturnal session. People began to dread the sound of the sticks. Someone said it was the fairies warning folk of a bereavement to allow them time to adjust to the sad event.

All this happened in the little County Down village of Saintfield over 50 years ago and for all that I know the hegging and whistling could still be going on.

Our house was haunted. It had an old fashioned range with the oven at the side. Our mum always had the kettle on the boil or a saucepan filled with soup or sometimes a piece of stewing meat with carrots and onions, simmering away. The stove was kept alight day and night for about six weeks after which Mum would let it go out completely, so that she could remove all the clinkers which could clog it up and prevent the fire burning properly. An old long black poker hung beside the fire. It was used to pull cinders away from the inside of the range.

One night I had gone to visit a friend and had come back quite late. My parents had gone to bed but had left the light on in the living room. As I passed the living room window I distinctly heard the sound of someone poking the fire. I came to the conclusion that Mum had got up and was attending it. The poking abruptly stopped as I opened the living room door. I shook myself. Nobody was about and the black poker was hanging in its usual place. I thought, 'Mum has just stepped out the back'. I went and looked. The back was in darkness. The rest of the family were in bed. I went to bed, forgot all about it and did not mention it to anyone.

About five weeks later I came home from a church social. Some of the family were still out and some were in bed. The fire was due to be cleaned out the next morning and it had cooled down. I heard nothing as I came in the door. I went straight up the stairs towards bed. I was about halfway up when I stopped in alarm. Someone was poking our fire. I forced myself to go downstairs and to look in the living room. The place was in darkness. I glanced at the black poker and swear it moved from side to side. I was scared so went upstairs to tell Da. He got out of bed and came downstairs as he thought a drunk might have wandered in and sat down for a rest. There was nobody there, or out the back as Da had a good look around.

There was no more poking for a couple of months. Then Billy and Mabel went to a dance and came home about 1.30 am. They heard the fire being poked and said they could actually hear the 'clink, clink' of the old poker on the bars of the range. It was indeed eerie.

We never solved the mystery of the poker and the stove. It was once said that the 'old folk', that is the old people who used to live in the house but who are long since dead, used to come out at night after everybody had gone to bed, sit by the fire and have crack. Perhaps the old folk associated with our old house poked the fire. I wonder where they have gone since the house was pulled down years ago?

Not all ghosts were frightening. Once I was very grateful to a guardian angel of a ghost I saw in a field.

One day I could not find my exercise book. I hunted and hunted for it until I was late and had to tell my two friends, Margaret and Susan, to go on without me. I knew better than

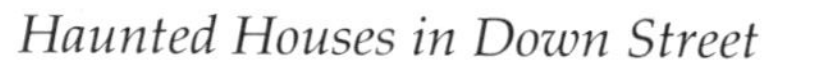

Haunted Houses in Down Street

face Miss Hay without my book and boy, was I relieved when I found it!

The old Public elementary school was situated between the Ballynahinch and Middle Roads. We had a choice of route. We could go via Main Street or we could go round by the garden hedges. There was a narrow path behind the hedges which meant walking in single file.

I ran out of the door just in time to see my friends climbing the steps leading to the path. I ran like mad but when I got to the beginning of the path I could just see Susan and Margaret in the distance, then they disappeared from sight.

I began to feel nervous. There was a bull grazing there and he was not always tied up. We knew about the bull but would rather face him than Miss Hay if we were late. The hedge was overgrown, so briars and thorns stuck into my face and neck as I tiptoed along. The only thing separating me from the bull was a thin wire net about four feet high. I glanced to my left. The big red bull was standing on the hill. He was not tied up and his nostrils were flaring. We had always been told not to wear red when walking the hedge path. I glanced at my clothing. Thank goodness only my socks were red and I did not think the bull could see them.

Just then the bull charged towards me. I knew I would not make it to the end of the lane and safety. I clutched my schoolbag tightly. My head thumped wildly. I was shaking. I could almost feel its breath as I listened to its heavy hooves pounding the ground, coming nearer and nearer. I pushed against the hedge, petrified, unable to move. I tore my shirt and red socks in the process but that seemed unimportant. I was terrified. I thought my time had come.

Then a strange thing happened. I glanced to my left. I could smell smoke and somehow I felt a presence. That is the only way I can describe it. I heard nothing, but as I looked I saw an elderly man just behind me. Was I glad to see him! He had on an old pair of tweed trousers, big brown boots and a long Harris tweed type of coat. He was a stranger to me. He was smoking a pipe and had a black thorn walking stick in his left hand. He had a stern but kindly face. He did not speak or smile, just indicated with his stick that I should carry on. I was speechless from fright and shock. I threw him a grateful look and carried on my way until I came to the end of the pathway. The old man passed me with a curt nod of his head and went on his way. I was still in a state of shock. Before I could thank him he had disappeared.

My friends were waiting for me at the corner. They were white with terror.

"Did you see the old man?" I asked.

"What old man?" they questioned.

"The old man who walked past you a minute ago," I replied.

"Don't be daft!" they replied. "There was no old man. We looked back to see if you were coming and saw the bull charging at you. There wasn't anything we could do. We looked for a grown-up to help. No-one was around. We saw you standing up the hedge. We thought you were a goner! Then you began to walk along the path again and the bull went back up the hill. Nobody was on the path but you.!"

I reckon the man was a guardian angel sent to protect me. I never saw him again but have often wondered who he was. Perhaps he lived and died in Saintfield, was visiting his old haunts, came across a child in distress and decided to help. Looking back I felt it was odd that he did not speak. All I can say is "Thank you, guardian angel!" and I still feel Saintfield is full of ghosts.

FATHER SHIELDS AND OTHER ECCENTRICS

Father Shields was a very eccentric person indeed. He had strong views and fixed ideas but he was a friend and councillor to every side of the community.

One day Father Shields went into the butcher's shop and asked for a bag of ribs. He was a difficult customer so when he appeared the staff scuttled away into the back out of sight and left the most junior member to deal with him. On this particular day there were quite a number of people in the shop. The assistant went into the back of the shop, returned and said, "We do not have any ribs." Father Shields addressed the shop's customers in his loud, sermon giving voice. "They are now trying to tell us that pigs no longer have ribs!" and hurried out none too pleased.

Father Shields had a mania about horses. He was a good judge of horse flesh who felt everyone should abandon motorised transport and return to the horse. One day he was cutting his hedges at Carrickmannan Cross Roads when a car approached from the direction of Raffrey. He ran out at the car in a rage with his pitch fork in his hand only to discover, to his acute embarrassment, it was the newly ordained minister of Raffrey Presbyterian Church.

Father Shields was an excellent business man. When he first arrived in the parish the priest's house was a long way from his church in Carrickmannan. He wanted to live near the church. Tom Mullan was a bachelor who lived on a farm at the cross roads convenient to the church. Father Shields arranged a swop with him for a holding of much less value on the Listodder Road. All this happened in the late 1920s and early 1930s.

Father Shields owned some houses in front of the chapel on Main Street. During the First World War he decided he wanted to raise the rent up in one of the houses so he would have to evict his tenant. She refused to go! One washing day he drove down into the yard and threw her washing into the mud. She still refused to move. The following washing day he was in the process of doing the same dirty trick when she caught him in action. She lifted a bucket of soapy water, which

Main Street, Father Shields lived in first house on left

had a scrubbing brush inside, and threw the contents around his reverence. He took her to court but lost the case.

I remember an occasion when the children had just been released from the Roman Catholic school in Comber Street. Some of the older boys ran ahead and reached Main Street at the end of the Square. They spotted Father Shields coming with his horse and cart. They turned towards the others and yelled a warning, "Here comes the old bugger. He will make you hold his horse!"

Mary was another eccentric. It could be awkward to meet her in a confined place, such as a shop. If anyone caught Mary's eye she cursed the offending person with vengeance and was capable of going on for a full five minutes without repeating herself.

Mary was good at pulling flax. One day she was busy pulling flax, on a farm a couple of miles outside Saintfield, with Matt McMullan and about three or four others, when they were called in for dinner. After the main course there was rice pudding. Some of the pudding was laced with laxative. They kept urging Mary to eat more and more helpings. Mary was greedy and obliged! When it was time to go back to work she was unable to move. All she could do was groan! The others managed to get her into Matt's donkey and cart and Matt had the job of transporting her home!

One of the farmer's wives travelled into Belfast to do her shopping and arrived back on the 5.15 pm train. She went into Minnis brothers' shop. She was absolutely laden with parcels and asked if she could leave them there while she went down the Street 'for a mouthful of tea'. After that she intended to go to a lecture in the Guild Hall beginning at 8 pm.

Sam told her he would be happy to oblige and would take care of her belongings until she returned. He made a few

David McKee grocer, Main Street

discreet inquiries and found she had bought an alarm clock. When she went for tea Sam wound the clock up and set the alarm for 8.45 pm. She picked up her belongings and made her way to the Guild Hall.

As the meeting went on some people were concentrating on what the speaker was saying, others were trying hard to stay awake while others had given up trying and were dozing. Suddenly there was a loud clanging and the place was in bedlam. The lady with the alarm clock had a very red face!

The actions of tricksters such as Sam and eccentrics such as Father Shields kept the neighbourhood in fireside crack.

THE WILD WORLD AT LAST

In 1948, at the grand old age of 14, I left school. Or, to put it another way, the teachers simply informed us our time was up and asked about the type of work which would interest us. There was no suggestion of further education. We were simply thrown out into the big wild world. At first I did not feel worried. The world was just waiting for someone with my ability to come along. Just think, I could be paid as much as £2–£3 a week! Any job would do. I was not fussy.

I gathered up 2 shillings for the return fare to Belfast and trailed factories. I remember going to the jam factory in East Belfast and getting a cool reception. "No!" they said, "We do not have a job for the likes of you." They did not even give me a jam buttie! Dispirited, I visited a few more factories, but the answer was always the same, "No! No work."

I arrived back in Saintfield disappointed and disillusioned. Next evening when Da had finished with the 'Belfast Telegraph' I picked it up and turned to the 'Situations Vacant' column. My eye fell on the list of domestics wanted. "That's it," I thought, reading down the column, "I could do that job!" It was for general domestic help, and there was a phone number. I took my last 2 pennies and went down the Crossgar Road to the phone box. The operator helped me obtain the number, the woman answered, I put my pennies in and pressed Button 'B', as one did in those days.

The woman I spoke to seemed all right. She asked if I was available to go to her house for an interview. I most certainly was! I told her I would be there next day but had no money for the fare. "Borrow the money from somebody," she said, "and I will give it back to you." Happiness!

I borrowed the train fare and a few extra pennies from Da. I asked Winnie to come with me. I did not tell my mother where we were going. We went down Station Road and caught the train. The old County Down railway stopped at Knock, a Belfast suburb. We got out and walked a long way to the house, but eventually we found it, walked up the drive and knocked the door. A large lady with bright red hair answered and said, "My name is Mrs. Twist." She took us into the big kitchen and gave us a big, thick, round oatmeal biscuit which she said she had made herself. It tasted lovely. We were impressed.

There was a big dog in a basket in the kitchen. Mrs. Twist said, "Do not speak to that dog. It might swallow you. It's very cross and doesn't respond to anyone, apart from Mr. Twist."

I had no intention of ever having anything to do with the dog. I was scared of him. I could see he did not like me. In the future I was to discover the dog lay in his basket all day and glared at me. He only went out into the garden to the toilet. Often he did not make it and I had to clean his pee and shit. If I was upstairs when the brute had an accident I was called down to remove the mess.

Anyway, Mrs Twist asked me when I could start. She wanted someone immediately as her other 'girl' had left. I said, "I can start straight away." I was anxious to get going. She showed me my room as the job was a 'live in' post. It looked luxurious to me! A bed to myself! I was told my wages were £1 a week, a roof over my head and my keep. What more could a body want? Opportunities like this do not come every day. I decided to start there and then. I did not need to go home to pack. I had the clothes I stood up in and a few pence. I had enough.

Then I remembered 12 year old Winnie standing in the background. "I'll take Winnie to the station and put her on the train, " I said, feeling very grown up, "Then all she will have to do is get out at Saintfield and walk up Station Road." I asked Winnie to tell my parents what had happened and told her to tell Da I would pay what I owed him when I got my first week's wages. I had borrowed half a crown.

At first I enjoyed having my own bed and use of a proper bathroom and toilet. Being young and naive, I thought it was very grand. A feeling of rebellion grew at the back of my mind as I became exhausted slaving from morning to night. I was on duty all day. I scrubbed floors, cooked meals, took the children to school and took them shopping, although they were only a few years younger than me. I had to call the girls Miss Mary and Miss Lucy while the boy was Master Ronald.

I was constantly reminded of my lowly position and felt resentment at having to address very ordinary people by formal titles. It was psychological cruelty beyond belief, designed to make the likes of me believe we were inferior. The family had their meals in the dining room while I ate what was left alone in the kitchen. "God," I often thought, as I avoided the evil eye of the bad tempered dog as it lay and glowered at me, "There must be something better in life than this!" I felt isolated.

The family had one large sitting room which was dominated by a grand piano. Whenever the family went out I used to sit at the piano and pretend to play and sing. I do not know what I was trying to prove, it was just something I wanted to do. It seemed like a luxury. A rare space to myself.

I had very little clothing and Mrs. Twist took it upon herself to make sure I did not freeze in the bitterly cold weather. She gave me one of her old coats. I thought it was wonderful! It was made of green and brown–herring bone tweed. She was a tall, well built woman and I was small, about 5 feet and weighed 7 stone, so the coat drowned me. I wore it proudly although its shoulders hung down around my elbows!

The only outing I had was when I went home once a week. I had to pay my bus fare out of my salary so had very little left to buy the necessities of life, such as clothes. I became terribly tired, felt I had no life of my own and was on the point of breaking when I decided I had had enough. I simply picked up my few belongings, walked out and never looked back.

I went and stayed with my Aunt in East Belfast. She had two children and a small 2 bedroomed house. I stayed the night and slept on the settee. My carrier bag, with all my belongings in it, sat on the floor beside me. Once more I consulted "The Belfast Telegraph" and obtained another job, this time off Belfast's Lisburn Road.

To my horror my new job was even worse than the previous one! The family consisted of a young couple with a baby. They took in lodgers and had the wife's mother living with them. Again I had to work very hard for minimal wages and my keep although I had one pound five shillings each week instead of one pound! There was very little food to eat so I was always hungry and had to use some of my wage to buy fruit, sweets and so on. Once again, the family ate in the dining room and

I was left alone in the kitchen with the dog. I ate off a small card table.

I remember one lodger with affection. She was a school teacher and a very nice person. She lit her fire when she came in from work and I spent time talking to her and helping her do odd chores. One day the wife's mother called me in and told me off. She said, "You are here to work for the family and it is not your place to be friendly with the lodgers!"

The mother was an unpleasant person, cynical, with inflated ideas about her station, and there would have been more warmth in an ice–cube. She made me wear an apron and a cap. One day my sister Mabel came to see me. She took one look and said, "For goodness sake, do not wear THAT HAT!" I must have looked like a pauper. I think the old mother enjoyed being seen to have a maid in a uniform. She used to send me out to the bread van, which came around the neighbourhood twice a week, to buy a soda farl and two Paris buns. I believe she did that to show the neighbours she had a domestic servant.

I was very unhappy. There was little peace for me in that house. I was constantly watched. The atmosphere was dreadful. My only pleasure was listening to 'The McCooeys' on the wireless. It was a very popular programme at the time and I particularly enjoyed the late James Young playing the part of Derek, the window cleaner.

I began to plot and scheme about how I could get out of this awful job. I knew I would be unwise to give notice because while I was working it my life would be made even more miserable. I decided not to look for another servant's job but to go home to Saintfield for a rest.

One morning I got up early while everyone was still in bed, had a cup of tea, gathered my few belongings together and began to walk down the Lisburn Road towards the Saintfield bus–stop in Ormeau Avenue. I felt as free as a bird, without a thought of the people I had just left. I met the kind teacher returning to the house. She had been away overnight and was returning to collect a few books before going to school. She stopped and spoke to me but I did not linger. I was in a hurry. I am sure she knew my intentions but she did not mention them. I was terrified in case I felt a hand on my shoulder dragging me back into service.

When I had been at home about a week our vicar came to see me. "Is it not the custom to give notice when you leave a job?" he asked. The vindictive old bat of a mother had got in touch with him! "I don't know," I replied meekly with my heart full of rage.

After a few days at home I decided to look for another job. I decided I could not face domestic service at the moment so went down to Comber Mill. The Mill did not take applications in the usual sense. Applicants travelled by bus and waited outside the manager's office until he came along. The interview was casual. References were not taken up and individuals were employed more or less on the spot. The strange thing about the mill was it was possible to be paid off on Friday and be given two weeks' wages as compensation, come back on Monday and get your job back again! Of course in this case it was necessary to work for two weeks before receiving any pay.

It has been said on numerous occasions that Comber Mill put many a one's dinner on the table. I agree but feel, in common with other mills, it also put many people in their graves. The conditions for employees, mostly women and girls, were terrible. There was no one to check up on the health and safety of the horrific conditions. The owners, to my knowledge, never visited the workers.

I worked in one of the flax rooms. The flax rooms were large and seemed airless. The nature of the work meant the windows had to stay closed so the air was dry and full of dust. It certainly was unhealthy. I felt ill most of the time I worked there. The female workforce were supervised by a foreman who seemed to spend most of his time walking round dressed in a white coat, looking as if he felt he had an elevated position. If I was not working in a flax room I was sent to another room where I had to stand in water all day. I do not know which was worse.

Workers were paid on Friday afternoon. Our salary was £2.4s a week. One of the office workers came into the room and we stood around in a circle until our names were called, then we went up and were given cash out of a tin box. There was no kind of formality like wage envelopes.

The work was not suited to me. It made me feel ill but I stayed in the job for about 8 months before finally deciding to leave, but this time, unlike service, I could put my notice in and not fear reprisals, although the world seemed big, wild and lonely.

THE GRAND INTERVIEW

I was ill when I left Comber Mill. Obviously the work did not agree with me. "I'd like to stay alive," I thought grimly to myself.

I stayed at home until I felt better. I had no money. I was conscious that my parents were paying for food for me out of their meagre resources. In those days there was no financial assistance, no health and social security, no dole or anything like that. If one was not fit to work one starved unless family and friends were in a position to help. I was not starving. I was just miserable. I was at a loose end. I could not afford to go to the cinema or buy anything. I had no money. Life looked bleak indeed. I could not bring myself to look for another live–in domestic service job. The ones I had left were too fresh in my mind.

One day, while visiting a neighbour, I heard the Mrs. Armytage Moore was looking for help in Rowallane. She was 'gentry'! At that time gentry seldom advertised for servants. Why should they? There was no need. There were plenty of girls only too willing to work for them and some folk considered it a privilege. The more I thought about working at Rowallane the more it appealed to me. I would have regular employment, a wage and I would be working for the nobility rather than the ordinary people who had once employed me.

One fine afternoon I set off for Rowallane via the back road. As I made my way past the rhododendrons, the lake and the monkey puzzle tree I wondered what my chances were. The house came into view and I walked round to the kitchen door and spoke to Agnes, the housekeeper. She said "Yes! More help is needed in the house. Sit down there and I will fetch Mrs. Armytage Moore." She was back within a few minutes saying, "Mrs. Armytage Moore is too busy to see you today. Can you come back next week?" We arranged a date.

I went home elated! I told my mother and anyone else I met!

On the appointed day I dressed in my best, to look as impressive as possible, and left home early to be in good time for my big interview. I returned to the kitchen door, was let in by Margaret, the house parlour maid, and taken to the servants sitting room to await the call from the mistress. Margaret came from Cork and was wearing a severe black dress with a small white muslin collar and with a narrow matching hairband and a small white starched afternoon apron. She wore black stockings and laced shoes. This was the afternoon attire for a servant in her position in the big house.

I sat on the hard sofa in the servants' room and looked around. The room was at the end of the kitchen. There was no fire. The heat from the kitchen range warmed the wall and that was felt to be sufficient. There was a square of lino and a small mat on the floor, two dining room chairs and a table in the middle.

Margaret came back and asked me to follow her as Madam was ready to see me now. We went out through the door into the dingy servants' hall, through another door into the main hall of the house. I blinked. I found it hard to believe I was in the same house. It was beautiful. There was a lovely pale blue carpet on the floor with a matching stair carpet. Such luxury!

We entered the drawing room. I heard the 'clip, clip' of our shoes as we walked on the polished wooden floor. I was feeling nervous now. What if she asked me about my previous jobs? We reached the study. Margaret half pushed me in through the door. It was dark as the heavy curtains were partly drawn. I stood like a mouse behind Margaret as she announced, "Madam, this is the girl who has come about the work."

The first thing I noticed was the strong smell of cigarette smoke. The air was full of it. The house parlour maid left the room and I moved slowly towards the middle. I could just make out a shape sitting in a large leather chair by the window. Madam was smoking a cigarette through a long green holder. I looked down at the floor and saw her big shoes. They were brown, held in place by a strap with a button at the side and they had white tips at the toe and the heel. They were elegant. I looked at her lisle stockings, then noticed she was wearing a fairly long pale blue chiffon dress with several chiffon scarves in different colours. I was fascinated. Her hair was fair and

Rowallane

Nora

piled up on the top of her head in tight little curls. She had a lot of make–up and strong perfume. She kept me standing throughout the interview.

Madam explained she had a cook, housekeeper, house parlour maid, a woman to come in twice a week and someone to come in once a month to do sewing and alterations. She was looking for a between maid, which I was to learn later was the worst position in a big house. She asked me my age and if I had any experience as a domestic servant. I explained I had worked at Knock then finished off my apprenticeship on the Lisburn Road. I was fully qualified in scrubbing, knowing it was necessary to scrub along the grain, in washing down walls, and in washing dishes starting with the saucers, then the cups, followed by the plates etc. I explained how I was fit to work in a grand house like Rowallane.

She broached the subject of wages. I replied that I felt two pounds and ten shillings was a suitable wage for a person of my experience and ability. She looked at me. "I was thinking more in the region of two pounds," she said, "But I will go up a shilling if you will come down."

"It's a deal!" I replied. "When do I start?"

"Go and see Agnes. She will sort out the details." She dismissed me with a wave of her cigarette holding hand so quite a whiff of smoke was sent in my direction.

Agnes arranged for me to start the following Monday. I rushed home to tell everyone my good news. This would be different from my previous experiences. I was to work for the elite, not the jumped up people who had once employed me. I was a success. I had been through a big interview!

WORKING FOR THE GENTRY

I was very happy the following Monday as I dressed and got ready to begin work in Rowallane. I had a quick cup of tea and set off down the street through the steady drizzle of rain. Work began at 8.00 am so I had to leave the house shortly after 7.40 am. Sometimes I was lucky and either a local farmer or Major Anderson who lived locally and who, along with his partner, owned Anderson and McCauley's in Belfast, gave me a lift. Lifts were rare so I usually legged it.

Agnes, the housekeeper, met me, showed me where to hang my coat, gave me a towel to dry my hair and set me down with a large slice of white fried bread and a cup of tea. I was hungry! Then I was set to perform my first task, scrub the front door step and clean the inner and outer halls. As I worked down on my knees sweet scents drifted in from the garden. I glanced to my left and admired the rich colours of the flowers peeping through the iron gate leading to the walled garden where pale yellow and mustard blended with strong blues and gentle pinks. Scrubbing the door step was pleasant during fine summer days and awful during the winter when I had to hack and scrape ice and snow away before I could start.

My next task was to clean Madam's bathroom. Ideal servants were expected to carry out their tasks without being either seen or heard by their masters. I carried cloths, cleaning fluid and brushes up the back stairs and listened for the sounds of Madam walking from the bathroom to the airing cupboard where she got dressed. She never wore slippers, just an old pair of saucer heeled shoes up stairs which she always changed before she came down. The shoes made a noise as she tramped over the carpet. I hurried past the airing cupboard. I had to be quick because Madam splashed a lot of water on the floor and if it was not wiped up quickly I had a hell of a job getting a shine on the lino. Madam expected perfection.

After I had cleaned and polished the bath room I gathered up my cleaning materials and went along to Madam's bedroom door to see if she had left any shoes outside to be cleaned. I took them down to the room next to the pantry and cleaned them later in the morning.

I was fascinated by Mrs. Moore's clothes. They felt so nice, so different from my own. I used to try her shoes on in secret. I thought they were wonderful! I wondered if they suited my feet, but as she took size 8 and I size 4 it was difficult to tell.

I came down stairs between 10.30 and 10.45 am. and went into the dining room to clear the dishes the master had used for breakfast from the table. If I was lucky there would be a slice of toast left which I could eat. I was constantly hungry! I made a big pot of tea and put cups and the few biscuits given to me by the housekeeper on the table.

John Hanvey and Eddie Hayes, the gardeners, joined us for our break. We enjoyed a good gossip as Eddie lived on the Lisburn Road in Saintfield and the housekeeper liked to hear all the latest news. Eventually Agnes would walk to the back door with the gardeners and stand there for ages while I cleared the table and then waited for her to return and tell me what to do next.

Every day I had to get down on my hands and knees and scrub the kitchen's red tiled floor. It was a large area and it took ages. I kept an anxious eye on the clock because at 12 pm Madam made her debut in the kitchen to discuss the menus for the following day. When she entered a chair was prepared for her to use, I did my best to look invisible, crept out to set about other cleaning tasks and closed the door. Planning menus was a highly charged and important daily event.

I set about cleaning Madam's shoes, then brushed the corridors and the cold room. In those days there were no fridges so many houses had a small dark windowless north facing room in which food was stored. In the summer months the sink was filled with cold water and containers of milk were stood in it to keep fresh.

Once the floors were swept I had to wash them, then sweep and clean the servant's quarters, including the bathroom and toilet. I came down in time to hear the click of the kitchen door as Madam swept in with never a glance or a word in my direction.

Rationing was still in operation during the 1950's so lunch was a meagre affair. The Armytage Moores usually had something like an egg on toast while the servants had bread and jam. The master and Madam never hurried any meal so by the time they had finished and we had cleared away it was usually about 2.30 pm.

At about this time Margaret, the house parlour maid, went up to her room for a rest and to change into her afternoon uniform. She came down just before 4 pm in time to serve afternoon tea.

In the meantime I had to prepare the vegetables for dinner. I had to undertake lengthy tasks such as peeling individual broad beans before they were placed on a serving dish and covered with white sauce. Agnes kept a stock pot on the side of the range so scraps of vegetables, spare onions, tomatoes and potatoes were put into it and left to simmer all day. Sometimes I had to sieve the contents of the stock pot. It took ages and there was no satisfaction in the job as servants were

Saintfield Cricket Club, circa 1954; including Colonel Perceval Price middle back row, Rev James Donnelly beside Colonel Price to right of picture, front row, 2nd left Bobby Walkinshaw, 2nd right, Andy Davidson, 2nd right Sam Davidson

not allowed to eat soup.

Another time consuming job was grinding coffee beans using a small hand operated machine. Servants were not allowed to drink coffee, only tea.

When the Armytage Moores had finished afternoon tea, cook usually wet a pot of tea in the kitchen. If the gardeners were working nearby they came in for a cup and a bit of crack, then checked to see if the master had left any shoes to be cleaned. When visitors visited Rowallane the chauffeurs came into the kitchen for refreshments. They always gave the impression they looked down on us. After all, they were capable of driving posh cars, but I do not think their employers rated them highly.

By now it was between 5 and 6 pm. Time to make dinner. This took a long time because the old range was very temperamental and cook had only one oven. She made a lot of sauces such as bread sauce and cheese sauce. This resulted in a lot of dirty utensils, pots and pans which I had to wash in the kitchen. Dirty cups, saucers, plates and silverware were washed in the pantry. I used to push the old sash window up, gaze out at the rhododendrons and dream of better times to come. Perhaps my Prince would come or I would earn the chance to become a nurse?

We started serving dinner about 7.30 pm. All meals were announced by striking a large gong. I always felt like Metro–Goldwyn Meyer announcing a film when I had to strike it! Dinner was a formal occasion with three or four courses, all properly served. The master and Madam loitered over their food. We could not serve a course until they rang for it. At long last they would inform the House Parlour Maid that they wanted coffee served in the drawing room where they sat and smoked and read until bed time.

There I was. Washing bloody dishes again. As I wiped the last pan, I breathed a sigh of relief. I was exhausted and ready for bed, but first I had to lay the fire so it could be relit first thing in the morning and then face the road home. My sister June used to come after school with her books and sit in the kitchen until I had finished my work. Many times we set the fire only to have it catch fire as the range had not cooled down sufficiently. We had to wait until sufficient time had passed to allow the fire to be laid. This meant we did not arrive home until late. There were few lights along the road. It was frightening because once we came out of the house it was so black we did not know where we were going. Walking in dense fog was terrifying as we would veer off the road. We could not afford to buy a torch to help us on our journey. June and I clung to each other, frightened, as we made our way down the road. There was a rock, called the Deals rock, on the right hand side of the road which acted as a landmark. Once we passed that we felt the worst of the journey was over.

I was very apprehensive if I had to walk home alone. I remember one night as I returned on my own I glanced behind and saw a man standing on the left of the road. He did not speak and neither did I but I was terrified!

Being a between maid in Rowallane was hard thankless work. I cannot say I enjoyed it but at least I had the support of my family and was able to return home each night.

ROYALTY VISITS ROWALLANE

One day we heard a rumour that we were to be visited by Queen Elizabeth the Queen Mother and her younger daughter, Princess Margaret Rose. The news caused great joy and excitement, but we did not know if it was true. Then Madam became even more house–proud than usual and we, the servants, gossiped about how we felt the rumour was correct. We spent weeks preparing the house while outdoors the gardeners worked themselves into a frenzy beyond belief. Madam told the housekeeper a few days before the expected visit and she told the rest of us. I thought I could burst with excitement!

The Royal party drove into Rowallane from the Belfast Road entrance and drove up the long drive. They arrived on a lovely warm sunny summer day and were greeted at the front door by the Armytage Moores. The servants hid behind the house outside the servants' quarters and peered round the wall at the royal guests or peeped out of the scullery window. We watched as Mr. Moore set off through the gardens with Queen Elizabeth followed by Princess Margaret, Mrs. Moore and the officials. We saw the Royals chatting away to the Moores and Mr. Moore, in particular, appeared in his element. He looked as if he was enjoying showing his rare trees, shrubs and herbaceous plants to the Queen who was both interested and knowledgeable. She asked a lot of questions and gestured every now and again with her hand, which was clearly visible because she was wearing white gloves. She wore a beautiful cornflower blue dress of a chiffon type material with a very full skirt and lovely wide elbow length sleeves. She had white, high heeled shoes with a smart matching handbag. I was filled with a strange emotion as I watched and my eyes filled with tears. The green of the lawn and the blue of her dress is something which has always stood out in my mind. The Queen was charming, as was Princess Margaret and they both took the time to notice the servants concealed in the pantry or peeping round the end of the house and to wave to us.

Princess Margaret was small and slim with fairly long dark brown hair. Madam towered over the princess, who was wearing a grey summer dress which reached just below her knees and was covered in a small flower pattern. I loved her shoes. They were fashionable, pink, leather sandals with a wedge heel and a thin ankle strap. She carried a little pink handbag to match her shoes. She had a lovely warm smile.

Walled garden Rowallane

Once the royal party had disappeared down the garden we returned to the servants' quarters. We felt very unsettled and excited. I was sent up to Mr. Moore's bedroom to watch for the Royal party's return to the house so that I could warn the housekeeper. I was practically trembling as I gazed through the window then, after about fifteen minutes, I spotted them trooping into the walled garden. I rushed down the stairs to tell Agnes so she could bring the orange and lemonade out of the cold room, put it into jugs and set it on the table for our royal guests.

The table was set with the best china and placed just under the window. It was covered in dainty sandwiches, biscuits and small cakes. Tea and coffee were provided as well as the orange and lemonade. Staff were not required to serve the royal guests as Mrs. Moore did that herself. We were disappointed not to be given the opportunity to be close to the queen and princess and to perhaps hear snatches of conversation and see what they ate. However, Eddie Hayes, one of the gardeners later told me he watched in through the window and neither of the royals ate anything. They just had a cold drink.

All too soon the royal visit was over with the Queen and Princess Margaret speeding their way back to Belfast. We had the impression that they had enjoyed themselves and I remember Mr. Moore describing afterwards about how the royal visitors had particularly enjoyed seeing and standing under the rare handkerchief tree.

I suspect the Queen Mother heard about Rowallane's wonderful garden from her elder sister, the Lady Rose, who later became the Countess of Grenville. Lady Rose and her husband visited Rowallane frequently. Lady Rose was in every way a true lady, small and quiet, always tastefully dressed with no sign of ostentation and she possessed great humanity. She always had a word for the servants, which we appreciated. She often asked me how I was and chatted to me about what I intended to do for a career. Once she expressed surprise on hearing that I was a member of such a large family.

King Leopold of Belgium also visited Rowallane. We did not hear any impending rumours about his visit but were simply told one night that he was visiting the following day. The study and drawing room were cleaned earlier than usual next morning and drinks glasses were set out along with cheese and biscuits.

This royal visit was very low key. The police were not in evidence and the king arrived when I was out at the side of the house. Naturally I peeped around the wall and saw a long, sleek, black car purring up the drive. It contained two people, the king and his uniformed driver. The king was a very tall man who wore a dark suit, white shirt and green tie. His shoes were black and very shiny. Madam was still upstairs but Mr. Moore came out of the door to greet his royal guest. They went off down the garden together and spent about one and a half hours there before going into the drawing room where Madam joined them.

The driver brought the car around to the back of the house and joined us for morning tea in the kitchen. He was a pleasant friendly man who apologized because he could not take us for a drive because he had to be available when the king was ready. However, we were invited to sit in it. "Whatever next?" I thought. "Here I am sitting in a limousine which belongs to a king. Working in Rowallane certainly has the occasional perk with its opportunity to spy on royalty!"

THE ARMYTAGE MOORES

When I went to work at Rowallane Mr. Armytage Moore was getting on in years. He was a nice kindly man with a keen sense of humour. He loved his gardens and spent hours supervising the work or just strolling around the grounds. At this time he employed two gardeners, John Hanvy and Eddie Hayes. They worked hard to keep the gardens immaculate and seemed to take as much pride in the place as the master.

The master had a natural ability to relate to people. He loved visits from bus parties and being in the middle of the crowds pointing out different trees and shrubs, talking about his travels to different parts of the world to procure plants. It

Mr & Mrs Armytage Moore

always gives me pleasure to visit a garden centre and see a plant proudly bearing the name Rowallane.

The master had a bath, in his own bathroom, every Thursday evening about 5 o'clock. The gardener used to go into his bedroom about 6 o'clock and cut his finger and toe nails when they were still soft after the bath. I suppose the master felt he would rather be pruned by one of his trusted gardeners than anyone else!

Once Mr. Armytage Moore gave me some money and asked me to go and buy 100 cigarettes for him. I ran quickly to Gildeas on the Main Street, bought the cigarettes then called in Down Street on the way back. Da was there. "What are you doing with all those cigarettes?" he asked. "They're for the master," I replied. "Did you get a receipt?" demanded Da. I confessed I had never even thought about it. Da made me go back down to the shop and get one. Was he being careful or did he know the gentry better than me?

I remember in 1951 Hugh Armytage Moore had accumulated a lot of old wine, whiskey and other types of bottles. He wanted rid of them so sent for Willie Sefton, who lived in Saintfield. Willie loaded all the bottles on to his old hand cart. "How much are you going to give me for them?" asked the master. His wife expressed dismay at him wanting payment. "These chaps make money out of bottles," stated the master and pocketed the few shillings Willie gave him.

Neither the master nor Madam ever cleaned their own shoes or galoshes. He brought his shoes down in the morning on the way to breakfast and left them in the cloakroom next to the butler's pantry where one of the gardeners cleaned and brought them back to his room.

Mrs. Armytage Moore was a tall, thin fair haired woman who was very conscious of her position in society. Her day began when Agnes, the cook, took a cup of tea up to her bedroom about 8.30 am. Her bedroom was a large airy room at the front of the house. Agnes then prepared Madam's breakfast, the juice of a fresh orange, toast, marmalade and tea, arranged on a linen cloth on a tray. Madam took her time and loitered over breakfast, put on her dressing gown and old shoes and walked flip, flop up the corridor into the bathroom, bathed, then carried her under clothes to the airing cupboard on the upstairs corridor, opened the door and dressed while I cleaned the bathroom. Once, as I scurried by her on my way to the bathroom, I decided to have a really good look. Madam was standing with her back to me and my boldness went unnoticed. She took off her dressing gown and put on her type of old fashioned bodice common at the time, laced herself into her stays, pulled up her thick lisle stockings, fastened them to her suspenders, then climbed into her knickers. They were voluminous, to put it mildly, made of a silvery blue silky material which shone softly and came down past her knees.

Rowallane was a cold drafty old house although it had central heating so the airing cupboard must have been a comforting place in which to dress.

Once she had donned her underclothing, Madam slipped back into her dressing gown and returned to her bedroom to don her outer clothes. By the time she had washed, dressed, fixed her hair and so on the morning was over. She never appeared downstairs until around noon at the earliest. Her idea of a morning's work was planning the menus for the next day.

A light lunch was served in the dining room about one o'clock. This was something like what they called Scotch woodcock, bacon cut up very fine, fried in the pan along with an onion. Then Agnes mixed in a few scrambled eggs, put it on toast and took it into the dining room on silver plates from which it was served. After lunch, which took about an hour, the Armytage Moores indulged in small talk, then Madam put on her outdoor shoes, or her galoshes if it was raining, and went down the garden to pick flowers to bring back and arrange, if she felt she had time, then proceeded to the dining room for afternoon tea at 4 o'clock.

Both the Armytage Moores smoked. At the time so did I! In those days the dangers of cigarette smoking went unrecognised. People thought smoking was good for the nerves. Once Madam, who always used a cigarette holder, left a half smoked cigarette in the living room. I pounced on it and went into the toilet for a secret puff. She sent for me about 10 o'clock at night. "What happened to my cigarette?" she asked, "I left a half smoked cigarette on the ashtray intending to finish it after dinner and it has disappeared."

"I am sorry Madam," I replied," I thought you had finished so I emptied the ashtray." I did not like telling lies but realised the truth would be rewarded with the sack.

Afternoon tea was served on trays, silver teapot and all. Agnes served and poured the tea as I was not considered to be sufficiently well trained or senior to do so. Afterwards Madam would perhaps arrange a few vases of flowers around the house, then go up to her bedroom to rest or write a letter. Occasionally she received a visitor but, unlike her husband, did not appear to enjoy people.

The next part of her day consisted of making preparations for dinner. Dinner was a formal occasion and the Armytage Moores always dressed although they seldom had company. They ate broad beans and french beans, vegetables which were forbidden to servants. We ate cabbage and turnips. Cauliflowers were grown at Rowallane. I thought they were large white plants with green leaves around them. Years later I discovered that a cauliflower is a vegetable.

Madam liked milk chocolate. She kept an ample supply and ate a bar every night but she never gave us share. Servant meals were frugal in the extreme and we were always hungry. Margaret and I used to sneak little morsels off the serving plates on the way to the dining room. Treats like chocolate were not given to servants. The only time Madam parted with a bar was to give one to the housekeeper to make a 'Chocolate Fool' for dessert. The chocolate was melted, added to whipped cream and the two ingredients were then whipped together. Needless to say this was another food forbidden to servants!

Dinner consisted of three or four courses, all properly served. Madam always ate a lot of fairy toast. It was made from bread cut wafer thin, toasted in the oven and served on a silver dish. Madam took a lot of butter with her toast.

Once I had to serve dinner. Cook was away on holiday and Madam hired a temporary cook called Mrs. Webb. To put it mildly, Mrs. Webb and Margaret, the house parlour maid, did not get on. There was a personality clash and the kitchen was filled with the banging of pots, pans and kitchen utensils. Margaret replied by dropping the heavy silver candle sticks as she cleaned them. I as a junior member of staff did not ask questions or make comment.

Things came to a head the day Margaret went up to change into her afternoon dress and Mrs. Webb also went up to her room. They bumped into each other! The house resounded with shouting and stamping of feet. Mesmerised, I continued cleaning in the kitchen. Eventually I heard Mrs. Webb shout, "I have worked in bigger and better houses than you. You are not trained. You have only worked for jumped up gentry. I have worked for Royalty!" A door banged. Silence. A few minutes later Mrs. Webb appeared and looked at the clock. There was less than an hour till afternoon tea.

After about half an hour I heard feet and the thud of a large case being bumped down the stairs. I peeped into the hall. There was Margaret, case in hand. "I'm off" she snarled "and if you had any sense you'd go too. I'm not going to be insulted by that old dragon!" With that she marched out of the back door and began lugging the heavy case down the Avenue to the Belfast Road to catch a bus.

Madam came into the kitchen and there was a hushed conversation which I did not catch. Mrs. Webb returned and said, "You will have to serve dinner tonight!" I nearly fainted. Mrs. Webb comforted me. "Don't worry. I'll help you set the table and tell you what to do." She made fancy butter pats and arranged the fairy toast as I looked on in shock.

Soon it was dinner time and I had to sound the gong. There was a small table in the dining room covered with a dark green blanket. Cook gave me two soup plates and soup in a tureen. I put them on top of the blanket then waited until the Armytage Moores sat down and indicated they were ready to be served. I took the lid off the tureen, poured soup into the plates and served it. That night it was clear and looked like dish water.

I returned to the kitchen to wait for them to ring the bell for the next course. I felt pleased with my elevated position, removed the plates on cue and took in the main course of beef olives, boiled potatoes, fresh garden peas and cauliflower cheese. I felt starving as I served but knew there would be little left.

The sweet course consisted of bottled plums served from a silver dish. Afterwards there were two plums left! Happiness! I carried the dish out of the dining room, ate the plums with my fingers and slipped the stones into my pocket then lifted the dish to my mouth and swallowed the sweet sticky juice. Boys a boys! It tasted great! I wiped my lips and returned to the kitchen to fetch coffee and biscuits. I was really pleased with myself. Mrs. Webb said, "Well done!" and I felt I could rise to higher things in service. I never did!

Sometimes the Armytage Moores had coffee taken down to the drawing room after their meal. There they sat and smoked, listened to music or wrote letters, then around ten or half past ten, they proceeded to their separate bedrooms. It always seemed to take Madam a good hour or so to get ready for bed.

Da collected rags for recycling. I can well remember finding a black skirt which had been discarded by Madam. I was delighted because I thought I could sew it and render it wearable. As I sat sewing the garment fell apart in my hands. The material was rotten. I made several attempts, then gave up disappointed. The skirt was fit for nothing apart from the rag bag. I should have known better because Madam had a sewing woman who came to the house about once a month to alter and mend clothes, mend bed linen, make curtains and so on. If the sewing woman could not save the skirt I had no chance at all!

During the day of the sewing woman's visit her meals were taken to her on a tray. She worked in a disused bedroom upstairs. It must have been a lonely life using the old treadle sewing machine set out for her and being denied all human contact. Sometimes she took work home to finish.

The senior servants wore a dark grey heavy duty dress in the morning with a large apron. In the afternoon they changed into a severe black dress with a muslin apron and small matching head band. Once, during the sewing woman's visit, Madam decided to be generous and deck out her staff. She ordered two afternoon dresses each for the housekeeper and the parlour maid. They were steel grey with long white sleeves and a little collar. I thought they looked awful but need not have worried. I was only the in between maid, not on public show, so did not qualify for a dress. I felt somehow let down.

Hugh Armytage Moore became very ill. A nurse was hired to look after him. She was a nice woman and very caring. The vicar, James Donnelly, visited him frequently and some people around Saintfield remarked how empty the Armytage Moore pew, with its blue velvet upholstery, looked on Sundays without him. He died in his own bedroom looking over his beloved wall garden. Afterwards my heart was no longer in my job and I left Saintfield to seek my fortune elsewhere. I went to an agency which had offices in Belfast in Donegal Pass. They kept a register of people who wanted to go into service in England and they obtained a job for me in an old people's home. There I was treated very kindly. Sometime later I learnt there was a shortage of nurses and I was encouraged to apply for training. I was accepted and my dream came true. I became a nurse and no longer lived up the Down Street.

Nora Davidson, nurse 1959